Report to the Chairman, Subcommittee on Energy and Water Development, Committee on Appropriations, U.S. Senate

June 2014

ADVANCED REACTOR RESEARCH

DOE Supports Multiple Technologies, but Actions Needed to Ensure a Prototype Is Built

June 2014

ADVANCED REACTOR RESEARCH

DOE Supports Multiple Technologies, but Actions Needed to Ensure a Prototype Is Built

Highlights of GAO-14-545, a report to the Chairman, Subcommittee on Energy and Water Development, Committee on Appropriations, U. S. Senate

Why GAO Did This Study

NE conducts R&D on advanced nuclear reactor technologies with multiple aims, including (1) improving the economic competitiveness of nuclear technology to ensure that nuclear power continues to play a role in meeting our nation's energy needs; (2) increasing safety; (3) minimizing the risk of nuclear proliferation and terrorism; and (4) addressing environmental challenges, such as reducing greenhouse gas emissions. External groups have been critical of NE for, among other things, how it prioritizes advanced reactor R&D.

GAO was asked to review NE's advanced reactor R&D efforts. This report (1) describes NE's approach to advanced nuclear reactor R&D and (2) examines how NE plans and prioritizes its advanced reactor R&D activities, including deploying an advanced reactor. GAO reviewed laws and reports concerning NE's efforts to develop advanced reactor technologies and interviewed NE officials and a nonprobability sample of companies developing such technology, selected because of their involvement with DOE's R&D efforts.

What GAO Recommends

To better prepare DOE to meet the requirement of EPAct 2005 to deploy the NGNP prototype reactor, GAO recommends that DOE develop a strategy for resuming the NGNP Project and provide a report to Congress updating the status of the project. DOE agreed in principle with GAO's first recommendation and respectfully disagreed with the second. GAO believes these recommendations remain valid as discussed in the report.

View GAO-14-545. For more information, contact Frank Rusco at (202) 512-3841 or ruscof@gao.gov.

What GAO Found

The Department of Energy's (DOE) Office of Nuclear Energy's (NE) approach to advanced reactor research and development (R&D) focuses on three reactor technologies—high-temperature gas-cooled reactors, sodium-cooled fast reactors, and fluoride-salt-cooled high-temperature reactors—but NE is also funding research into other advanced reactor technologies. NE's approach is to conduct research in support of multiple advanced reactor technologies, while collaborating with industry and academia, with the ultimate goal for industry to take the results of NE's research to the next step of development and commercialization. This approach provides several advantages, including flexibility in responding to changes in future U.S. energy policy. Many representatives that GAO talked to from the nuclear power industry and the National Academy of Sciences agree with NE's approach, saying that current policies on controlling greenhouse gas emissions and disposing of nuclear waste do not make a compelling case for choosing a reactor technology to develop. However, others GAO talked to are critical of some of the reactor technologies NE chooses to research, citing economic and technological challenges. The Nuclear Energy Advisory Committee has criticized NE's approach, recommending that NE focus its efforts on a smaller number of technologies to help ensure that a reactor prototype is deployed. To remain aware of industry's R&D needs and international nuclear energy developments, NE regularly collaborates with industry and international organizations.

NE uses internal and external reviews to set program and funding priorities for advanced reactor R&D activities and to evaluate progress toward program goals. For example, NE conducts internal monthly and quarterly reviews to discuss project status, budgets, and technical highlights. Furthermore, NE's R&D efforts are periodically reviewed by external entities, including the Nuclear Energy Advisory Committee. Among the advanced reactor technologies that NE's R&D currently supports, the high-temperature gas-cooled reactor is the technology that is most likely to be deployed and commercialized in the near term, according to an NE planning document. NE officials said this likelihood is based on the wide range of potential industry market applications and because of substantial government investments in the technology's development. NE has been pursuing this technology under the Next Generation Nuclear Plant (NGNP) Project, as established by the Energy Policy Act of 2005 (EPAct 2005). Under EPAct 2005, DOE is to deploy a prototype reactor for NGNP by the end of fiscal year 2021. However, in 2011, DOE decided not to proceed with the deployment phase of this project, citing several barriers. For example, NE and industry have been unable to reach an agreement on a cost-share arrangement to fund the deployment phase because of a disagreement on the applicable cost-share levels and how and when the cost-share would be applied to specific activities or project phases. Although NE continues to conduct R&D for the NGNP Project, it has not developed a strategy to overcome the cost-share issue and other barriers to resuming the deployment phase of the project. Furthermore, DOE has not selected initial reactor design parameters or reported to Congress on an alternative date for making this selection. Without doing so, it is not clear when NE is going to take this next step in deploying the NGNP prototype reactor and it risks the project not being completed by the targeted date in 2021.

_____ **United States Government Accountability Office**

Contents

Abbreviations

DOE	Department of Energy
EPAct 2005	Energy Policy Act of 2005
FACA	Federal Advisory Committee Act
NE	Office of Nuclear Energy
NGNP	Next Generation Nuclear Plant
NRC	Nuclear Regulatory Commission
OECD	Organisation for Economic Co-operation and Development
R&D	research and development

GAO U.S. GOVERNMENT ACCOUNTABILITY OFFICE

441 G St. N.W.
Washington, DC 20548

June 23, 2014

The Honorable Dianne Feinstein
Chairman
Subcommittee on Energy and Water Development
Committee on Appropriations
United States Senate

Dear Madam Chairman:

Energy demand in the United States is expected to continue to grow over the coming decades, according to the U.S. Energy Information Administration, and energy security and greenhouse gas emissions from the burning of fossil fuels will continue to be of serious concern. Nuclear energy accounts for about 20 percent of electricity generation in the United States and produces no air pollution or greenhouse gases. However, the United States faces several challenges in developing additional nuclear energy facilities. For example, the March 2011 accident at Japan's Fukushima Daiichi commercial nuclear power plant has increased concerns about the safe operation of nuclear power plants worldwide. In addition, many uncertainties surround long-term storage and disposal options for spent nuclear fuel from existing power plants.[1] Spent nuclear fuel is considered one of the most hazardous substances on earth, and exposure can cause environmental harm and long-term health hazards, such as cancer, in those who are exposed to it. Spent nuclear fuel also raises concerns over nuclear proliferation and terrorism.[2] Specifically, concerns exist that terrorist networks could divert nuclear material intended for peaceful purposes to the development of nuclear weapons. In addition, the cost of developing, deploying, and operating

---

[1]Spent (or used) nuclear fuel—fuel that has been used in a reactor and removed from the reactor core—from light water reactors in the United States is currently stored at nuclear reactor sites around the country. About three-quarters of the fuel is stored in pools of water, and about one-quarter is stored in dry storage casks. For more information, see GAO, *Spent Nuclear Fuel: Accumulating Quantities at Commercial Reactors Present Storage and Other Challenges*, GAO-12-797 (Washington, D.C.: Aug. 15, 2012).

[2]Consistent with the Treaty on Nonproliferation of Nuclear Weapons, nuclear proliferation includes the transfer of nuclear weapons, related technology, or special fissionable material to nonnuclear weapons states. One factor contributing to the risks of nuclear proliferation and terrorism is the challenge of protecting spent nuclear fuel from diversion and theft.

new nuclear power facilities in the United States, relative to other types of energy sources, has been an impediment to increasing nuclear production.

Research on a new generation of advanced nuclear reactors, which are intended to improve on the current generation of nuclear reactors through increased safety, improved economic competitiveness, and reduced nuclear waste, is being conducted by governments and private industry around the world. In the United States, the Department of Energy (DOE) spends more than $80 million per year to develop advanced nuclear reactors with the aim of eventually replacing aging U.S. commercial light water reactors,[3] many of which are operating past the end of their initial 40-year operating period under renewed operating licenses.[4] DOE's Office of Nuclear Energy (NE) conducts research and development (R&D) on advanced reactors with multiple aims, including (1) improving the economic competitiveness of nuclear energy to ensure that nuclear energy continues to play a role in meeting our nation's energy needs, (2) increasing safety, (3) minimizing the risks of nuclear proliferation and terrorism, and (4) addressing environmental challenges such as reducing greenhouse gas emissions.[5]

In September 2006, we reported on NE's progress in deploying an advanced reactor prototype,[6] stating that initial R&D results were favorable, but DOE officials considered the schedule to be challenging,

[3]Light water reactors, also called Generation-II and Generation-III reactors, use ordinary (i.e., "light") water, either pressurized or boiling, for reactor moderation and cooling of the reactor core. Advanced reactors, also called Generation-IV reactors, use substances such as liquid metals or high-temperature gases to cool the reactor core. A moderator in a nuclear reactor is a substance that reduces the speed of the fast neutrons to better sustain the nuclear reaction. For more technical details of reactor types, see appendix I.

[4]For these reactors to continue operating, their owners must renew their licenses with the Nuclear Regulatory Commission (NRC), the federal agency responsible for licensing and regulating civilian nuclear reactors. In general, NRC licenses reactors to operate for 40 years and allows reactor owners to apply to renew their operating licenses for up to an additional 20 years per renewal. As of April 2014, 72 of the 100 currently operating commercial nuclear power reactors in the United States are operating with renewed operating licenses.

[5]The U.S. administration's goal is to reduce greenhouse gas emission levels by 83 percent of 2005 levels by the year 2050.

[6]GAO, *Nuclear Energy: Status of DOE's Effort to Develop the Next Generation Nuclear Plant,* GAO-06-1056 (Washington, D.C.: Sept. 20, 2006).

given the amount of R&D that remained to be conducted. External groups, such as the Nuclear Energy Advisory Committee,[7] the National Academy of Sciences, and we have reported on NE's advanced nuclear reactor R&D efforts from 2008 to 2013.[8] These reports have been critical of how NE prioritizes its advanced reactor R&D, the advanced reactor technologies that NE has chosen to fund, and how NE partners with industry to advance program goals.

In this context, you asked us to review NE's advanced reactor R&D efforts. Our objectives were to (1) describe NE's approach to advanced reactor R&D and (2) examine how NE plans and prioritizes its advanced reactor R&D activities, including deploying an advanced reactor prototype.

To address these objectives, we reviewed relevant federal laws and regulations, as well as reports by DOE, us, and others that describe NE's efforts to develop advanced reactor technologies. In addition, to better understand NE's approach to and decision-making processes for advanced reactor R&D, we interviewed NE officials; representatives from a nonprobability sample of companies developing advanced reactor technology;[9] knowledgeable members of the Nuclear Energy Advisory Committee and the National Academy of Sciences' National Research

---

[7]The Nuclear Energy Advisory Committee includes representatives from universities, industry, foreign nationals, and national laboratories. The committee paid particular attention to obtaining a diverse membership with a balance of disciplines, interests, experiences, points of view, and geography. The committee operates in accordance with the Federal Advisory Committee Act (FACA) and all applicable FACA amendments, federal regulations, and Executive Orders.

[8]See, for example, Nuclear Energy Advisory Committee, *Report to Nuclear Energy Advisory Committee Fuel Cycle Subcommittee Meeting of April 23, 2013* (Washington, D.C.: June 13, 2013); GAO, *Nuclear Fuel Cycle Options: DOE Needs to Enhance Planning for Technology Assessment and Collaboration with Industry and Other Countries,* GAO-12-70 (Washington, D.C.: Oct. 17, 2011); GAO, *Global Nuclear Energy Partnership: DOE Should Reassess Its Approach to Designing and Building Spent Nuclear Fuel Recycling Facilities,* GAO-08-483 (Washington, D.C.: Apr. 22, 2008); National Academies Press, *Review of DOE's Nuclear Energy Research and Development Program* (Washington, D.C.: 2008).

[9]Because this was a nonprobability sample, the information gathered from these companies cannot be generalized to the nuclear power industry as a whole, but it can provide illustrative examples. Based on our review of companies developing advanced reactor technology, we selected these companies because they had involvement with DOE's advanced reactor R&D efforts.

Council; and representatives from industry groups, including the Next Generation Nuclear Plant Industry Alliance and the Nuclear Energy Institute.[10] In addition, we visited two of DOE's national laboratories—Oak Ridge National Laboratory and Idaho National Laboratory—to better understand NE's R&D activities for advanced nuclear reactors. To select these laboratories, we analyzed the appropriated funding levels associated with NE across the 10 national laboratories that NE funds.[11] We selected the 2 laboratories with the highest levels of funding dedicated to NE programs over the past 5 years.

We conducted this performance audit from August 2013 to June 2014 in accordance with generally accepted government auditing standards. Those standards require that we plan and perform the audit to obtain sufficient, appropriate evidence to provide a reasonable basis for our findings and conclusions based on our audit objectives. We believe that the evidence obtained provides a reasonable basis for our findings and conclusions based on our audit objectives.

Background

According to its 2010 *Nuclear Energy Research and Development Roadmap: A Report to Congress*, NE's primary mission is to advance nuclear power as a resource capable of meeting the nation's energy supply, environmental, and energy security needs by resolving technical, cost, safety, proliferation resistance, and security barriers through research, development, and demonstration, as appropriate. NE conducts research aimed at (1) improving the reliability, sustaining the safety, and

---

[10]The Nuclear Energy Advisory Committee provides independent advice to the Office of Nuclear Energy on complex science and technical issues that arise in the planning, managing, and implementation of DOE's nuclear energy program. The National Research Council's mission is to improve government decision making and public policy, increase public understanding, and promote the acquisition and dissemination of knowledge in matters involving science, engineering, technology, and health. The Next Generation Nuclear Plant Industry Alliance is an alliance of nuclear technology companies, electric utilities, and industrial end users that seek to support efforts to design, build, operate, and use high-temperature gas-cooled reactors. The Nuclear Energy Institute develops policy on legislative and regulatory issues affecting the nuclear industry and serves as the nuclear industry's voice before the U.S. Congress, executive branch agencies, and federal regulators.

[11]The DOE Office of Nuclear Energy provides funding to 10 national laboratories: (1) Argonne, (2) Brookhaven, (3) Idaho, (4) Lawrence Berkeley, (5) Lawrence Livermore, (6) Los Alamos, (7) Oak Ridge, (8) Pacific Northwest, (9) Sandia, and (10) Savannah River.

extending the operational lifetime of existing light water nuclear reactors; (2) supporting the development of the next generation of nuclear reactors, including light-water-reactor-based small modular reactors and advanced reactors, with a focus on affordability; (3) developing sustainable nuclear fuel cycles; and (4) reducing the risk of nuclear proliferation and terrorism. Light-water-reactor-based small modular reactors are smaller in size and energy output than conventional light water reactors—but use the same basic technology for the nuclear reactor core—and offer several potential advantages over existing light water reactors, including lower capital and construction costs through factory fabrication; enhanced safety and security; improved operation times and longer life cycles; and flexibility to be sited at locations that cannot support large nuclear plants, such as isolated areas or sites with limited water supplies.

Advanced reactors, including advanced small modular reactors, use innovative nuclear fuels, coolants, and energy systems, and offer the potential for significant advantages over existing light water reactors, including greater energy conversion efficiency, reduced plant size, lower construction and operation costs, and improved safety. NE has mainly conducted advanced reactor R&D on high-temperature reactors and fast reactors. High-temperature reactors produce electricity, as well as process heat that can be used for industrial purposes, such as refining petroleum or producing hydrogen, and replace current sources of process heat from burning natural gas or other fossil fuels, which emit greenhouse gases. Fast reactors can use spent nuclear fuel as their fuel source, which reduces the need for long-term storage of spent nuclear fuel, and would more efficiently use uranium, helping reduce nuclear waste.

NE conducts nuclear reactor R&D through its Reactor Concepts Research, Development, and Demonstration program, which aims to (1) help advance nuclear power as a resource capable of meeting the nation's energy, environmental, and national security needs and (2) develop new and advanced reactor designs and technologies that advance the state of reactor technology and improve the economic competitiveness of nuclear power. The program encompasses the following subprograms:

- The Light Water Reactor Sustainability subprogram is developing the scientific basis to extend existing nuclear power plant operating life beyond the current licensing period and ensure their long-term reliability, productivity, safety, and security. This subprogram conducts research into materials aging and degradation, updating instrumentation and controls, and assessing reactor safety margins, among other things.

- The Advanced Reactor Concepts subprogram[12] supports the development of innovative reactor technologies that may offer improved safety, functionality and affordability; more efficient energy conversion; increased proliferation resistance and security; and that build upon existing nuclear technology and operating experience. It supports research to reduce technical barriers for advanced nuclear energy systems, and its efforts support various reactor technologies at different maturity levels.

- The Advanced Small Modular Reactor subprogram[13] supports the development of innovative small modular reactor designs that potentially offer improved safety, functionality, and affordability; more efficient energy conversion; increased proliferation resistance and security; and simplified operation and maintenance. For example, the program supports research into novel sensors and control systems for multiple reactor units, as well as advanced materials development.

Other NE programs conduct R&D that supports the nuclear reactor R&D efforts. The Fuel Cycle R&D program—which is primarily responsible for developing sustainable nuclear fuel cycles,[14] innovative processes to recover uranium from spent nuclear fuel, and nuclear fuel storage options—also supports existing reactors by developing accident-tolerant fuel and advanced reactors by developing advanced proliferation-resistant fuels.[15] The Nuclear Energy Enabling Technologies program conducts R&D on technologies that directly support and complement NE's advanced reactor and fuel cycle R&D efforts. This program

---

[12]The Advanced Reactor Concepts subprogram will be renamed the Advanced Reactor Technologies subprogram beginning in fiscal year 2015.

[13]Beginning in fiscal year 2015, the Advanced Small Modular Reactor subprogram will be consolidated into the Advanced Reactor Technologies subprogram.

[14]Sustainable fuel cycle options are those that would better utilize uranium resources, maximize energy generation, minimize waste generation, improve safety, and limit proliferation and terrorism risks, according to DOE.

[15]Accident-tolerant fuels are fuels that offer improved reliability and safety characteristics during accident conditions. Proliferation-resistant fuels are those that would make it more difficult or time-consuming to weaponize.

coordinates R&D on common issues and challenges that confront other NE R&D efforts to avoid duplication of effort.[16]

NE conducts most of this research at 10 DOE national laboratories across the country and, over the past 3 years, has spent an average of about $840 million per year on its mission to advance nuclear power (see table 1).[17] Of this amount, NE provides about $50 million annually to engage U.S. universities through its Nuclear Energy University Program to fund R&D and to build infrastructure and capabilities to enhance universities' ability to perform research and educate students.[18]

Table 1: Total Funding for DOE Office of Nuclear Energy (NE), Fiscal Years 2012 through 2014

Dollars in millions

Program	Fiscal year 2012	Fiscal year 2013	Fiscal year 2014
Fuel Cycle Research and Development	$181.0	$169.9	$186.2
Nuclear Energy Enabling Technologies	71.3	67.9	71.1
Reactor Concepts Research, Development, and Demonstration	110.7	104.8	112.8
Small Modular Reactor Licensing Technical Support	67.0	62.7	110.0
Other NE programs, transfer from Department of State, and use of prior year balances[a]	423. 9[b]	393.0[b]	397.4
Total	**$853.8**	**$798.3**	**$877.5**

Source: DOE. | GAO-14-545

[16]In addition to these programs, NE funds programs that coordinate its international activities, manage and protect its facilities, and provide overall direction and execution of NE's programs.

[17]NE conducts most of the advanced nuclear R&D at DOE's national laboratories, but some NE-funded R&D is carried out at university laboratories, and some is done by private industry through cooperative agreements.

[18]NE's Nuclear Energy University Program was established in 2009 to consolidate university support under one initiative and better integrate university research within NE technical programs. The mission of the Nuclear Energy University Program is to engage U.S. universities in conducting R&D that supports DOE's mission, improving related infrastructure, and supporting student education.

Note: Numbers may not add to total due to rounding.

[a]Other NE programs include facilities management, international cooperation, the Idaho Sitewide Safeguards and Security program, the Integrated University Program, and overall direction and execution of the Office of Nuclear Energy programs. The Integrated University Program funding is intended to support nuclear science and engineering by funding scholarships and fellowships in nuclear energy related fields of study, among other things. These funding levels also include funds transferred from the Department of State, funds transferred to the Small Business Innovation Research and Small Business Technology Transfer programs outside of NE, and the use of NE's prior year balance.

[b]The Idaho Sitewide Safeguards and Security program was funded within Other Defense Activities for fiscal years 2012 and 2013, but are reflected this table. The program was funded within NE for fiscal year 2014. Other Defense Activities funds elements that relate to and support the defense oriented activities within DOE.

NE's recent advanced reactor R&D efforts began in 2000, when NE convened a group of senior governmental officials from nine countries to discuss the development of such reactors in the United States and internationally.[19] This group, called the Generation-IV International Forum, and the Nuclear Energy Advisory Committee produced a Technology Roadmap for Generation-IV Nuclear Energy Systems in 2002. The intent of the forum was to develop competitively priced and reliable nuclear reactors, while satisfactorily addressing nuclear safety, waste, and proliferation concerns. In response to these efforts, the United States determined that it would fund the development of a high-temperature gas-cooled reactor as its top priority.[20] In addition, NE funded research into sodium-cooled fast reactors—fast reactors that use sodium

---

[19]As of January 2014, the 13 participating members were Argentina, Brazil, Canada, China, Euratom (the implementing organization for development of nuclear energy within the European Union), France, Japan, Russia, South Korea, South Africa, Switzerland, the United Kingdom, and the United States, according to the Organisation for Economic Co-operation and Development (OECD).

[20]The high-temperature gas-cooled reactor is an underground helium-cooled nuclear reactor technology. The reactor and the nuclear heat supply system consist of three major components: the reactor, a heat transport system, and a cross vessel that routes the helium between the reactor and the heat transport system.

to cool the reactor core—as well as a variety of other advanced reactors.[21]

The Energy Policy Act of 2005 (EPAct 2005) established in law the Next Generation Nuclear Plant (NGNP) Project.[22] The purpose of the NGNP is to develop a prototype reactor using advanced technology to generate electricity, hydrogen, or both. The law states that the NGNP Project shall consist of research, development, design, construction, and operation of a nuclear reactor prototype, and specifies completion dates for the project's two phases, as well as certain other requirements, including licensing. Specifically, EPAct 2005 states that Phase 1 of the project, which requires DOE to, among other things, conduct R&D activities enabling it to select and validate an appropriate technology, culminating in the selection of a technology and initial design parameters, by a target date of September 30, 2011. The law also authorized DOE to submit a report to Congress identifying an alternative date upon which the agency would select the technology and initial design parameters. Phase 2 of the project, in which DOE would develop a final design for a nuclear reactor prototype, apply for licenses to construct and operate the reactor technology, construct the prototype, and begin operations, is to be completed by a target date of September 30, 2021, although DOE is again authorized to submit a report establishing an alternate date for completion. EPAct 2005 also mandated the organization of a consortium of appropriate industrial partners that will carry out cost-shared R&D, as well as design, construction, and operation on behalf of the NGNP Project, and that the NGNP prototype reactor be located at the Idaho National Laboratory in Idaho Falls, Idaho.

---

[21]Advanced reactors have been built and tested in countries around the world, including in the United States, since the 1950s. Sodium-cooled fast reactors have been built and operated for research and commercial purposes in countries around the world, including France, Japan, Germany, Russia, the United Kingdom, and the United States. Two notable U.S. fast reactors include the Experimental Breeder Reactor, operational from 1964 through 1994 and the Fast Flux Test Facility, operational from 1982 to 1992. High-temperature gas-cooled reactors have also been built and operated around the world, including two that were licensed and operated in the United States. One reactor—Peach Bottom Atomic Power Station, Unit 1—was located in Pennsylvania and operated from 1967 to 1974, according to the U.S. Nuclear Regulatory Commission. The other—Fort St. Vrain Generating Station—was located in Colorado and operated between 1979 and 1989.

[22]Pub. L. No. 109-58, §§ 641-45, 119 Stat. 594, 794-99 (2005) (codified at 42 U.S.C. §§ 16021-16025).

In February 2006, the Nuclear Energy Advisory Committee recommended accelerating the NGNP Project schedule to, among other things, make the project more attractive to industry.[23] However, also in February 2006, the administration announced the newly formed Global Nuclear Energy Partnership program, which sought to encourage the expansion of nuclear energy while addressing the burden of spent fuel disposal and the risk of nuclear weapons proliferation and, according to a 2008 National Academy of Sciences report, led to reduced funding for the NGNP Project. Under the Global Nuclear Energy Partnership program, DOE focused advanced reactor R&D activities on developing sodium-cooled fast reactors, and it changed its approach from designing and building a small engineering-scale demonstration of the reactor and reprocessing facility, led by DOE's national laboratories, to accelerating its work with industry to demonstrate commercially viable sodium-cooled fast reactor technology in full-scale facilities.[24]

In 2008, we reviewed NE's Global Nuclear Energy Partnership program and found that DOE's original approach to the domestic component of the program—building engineering-scale facilities—would meet the program's objectives if the advanced spent nuclear fuel recycling technologies on which it focused could be successfully developed and commercialized.[25] However, we also reported that the approach lacked industry participation—potentially reducing the prospects for eventual commercialization of the technologies. NE favored an accelerated approach of building full-scale facilities that would likely require using unproven evolutions of existing technologies that would reduce the long-term benefits of the sodium-cooled fast reactor.[26] We recommended that NE reassess its preference for an accelerated approach. In response, DOE decided, in 2009, to no longer pursue the Global Nuclear Energy Partnership program. However, NE continued research related to sodium-

---

[23]Nuclear Energy Research Advisory Committee, *A Review of the NGNP Project* (Feb. 22, 2006).

[24]Engineering-scale demonstrations typically precede commercial-scale deployment and are meant to ensure technologies work as intended before an investment is made in a larger plant.

[25]GAO-08-483.

[26]Under the accelerated approach, DOE would partner with industry and use the latest commercially available technology to design and build a commercial-scale reprocessing plant and advanced reactor without first building engineering-scale facilities.

cooled fast reactors, with a new focus on long-term R&D coordinated with NE's fuel cycle research.

Also in 2008, the National Academy of Sciences' National Research Council issued a report reviewing NE's R&D efforts and concluded that the success of any particular advanced reactor technology in the United States would depend on policy decisions and other factors beyond NE's control.[27] In addition, the report concluded that NE's resources were barely adequate for basic studies related to the NGNP Project and entirely inadequate for (1) exploring the sodium-cooled fast reactor at a research level and (2) investigating other reactor technologies. The report also stated that selecting a specific technology to develop from among the options known at that time would have been premature.

In April 2010, NE issued its *Nuclear Energy Research and Development Roadmap: A Report to Congress*, which provides a basis to guide NE's internal programmatic and strategic planning for research going forward. Also in April 2010, NE issued *Next Generation Nuclear Plant: A Report to Congress*, which presents the historical background of the project; details the project's spending; and discusses the principal investments in design, licensing, and research. As discussed in this report, NE selected the high-temperature gas-cooled reactor as the advanced reactor technology to develop under the NGNP Project.

In its 2011 Phase 1 review of the project, the Nuclear Energy Advisory Committee reported that the NGNP Project was not ready to proceed to the complete set of Phase 2 activities, citing

- the need for more detailed design and R&D;
- the need to resolve key licensing issues;
- constraints imposed by EPAct 2005, such as the Idaho site requirement;
- the absence of a public-private partnership, as required;
- absence of industrial partners willing to commit to share in the cost of constructing the prototype reactor; and
- an unrealistic project plan given the limited amount of conceptual design work completed.

---

[27]National Research Council, *Review of DOE's Nuclear Energy Research and Development Program* (2008).

The committee recommended that NE continue conducting its Phase 1 R&D, focused on one technology and completing design work, initiate the partnership with the nuclear industry, and continue to engage the Nuclear Regulatory Commission (NRC)—the federal agency that licenses and regulates the nation's civilian use of nuclear reactors—to ensure that the regulatory framework for this new reactor technology would be ready to support commercialization. The committee also recommended eliminating the requirement that the NGNP prototype be sited at Idaho National Laboratory.

In October 2011, DOE submitted a letter to Congress in response to EPAct 2005 requirements to transmit the committee's report and to report on certain requirements to complete Phase 1 of the NGNP Project. As noted above, EPAct 2005 required, by September 30, 2011, that DOE select technology and initial design parameters; alternately, DOE was to submit a report to Congress identifying a new date upon which the agency would do so. In the 2011 letter, DOE stated that it was notifying Congress that the department had not selected the initial design parameters for the NGNP by September 30, 2011, and that it would not proceed with Phase 2 design activities at that time. The letter also stated that DOE would focus on remaining applied R&D, work with NRC on licensing framework, and establish the public-private partnership—in essence, to follow most of the advisory committee's recommendations—until conditions favorable to completing the NGNP Project warranted a change in direction. Further, DOE asserted that the partnership—rather than DOE—would select initial design parameters and would provide an update to the project's schedule and milestones.

In its fiscal year 2014 budget request to Congress, DOE indicated that NE would continue to fund some NGNP research activities under the Advanced Reactor Concepts subprogram.

NE's Approach to Advanced Reactor R&D Supports Several Advanced Reactor Technologies

NE's approach to its advanced reactor R&D is to support research on technologies associated with three main types of advanced reactors: high-temperature gas-cooled reactors; liquid-metal-cooled fast reactors, including the sodium-cooled fast reactor; and fluoride-salt-cooled high-temperature reactors. NE also conducts research supporting other less-developed advanced reactor technologies and supports the development of advanced small modular reactors. NE's approach to advanced reactor R&D addresses broad programmatic goals—including improvements in the economics, safety, and proliferation resistance of nuclear power plants—and aims to develop technologies to reduce nuclear waste and greenhouse gas emissions. This approach provides several advantages, including flexibility in responding to changes in future U.S. energy policy or other circumstances.

NE's Advanced Reactor R&D Efforts Are Focused on Three Primary Reactor Technologies

NE's approach to its advanced reactor R&D efforts primarily is to support research on three main advanced reactor technologies: high-temperature gas-cooled reactors; liquid-metal cooled fast reactors, including the sodium-cooled fast reactor; and fluoride-salt-cooled high-temperature reactors. On a smaller scale, NE also conducts or funds research supporting other less-developed advanced reactor technologies. In addition, NE conducts research supporting a variety of technologies related to the development of advanced small modular reactors. In discussions with representatives from the nuclear industry, members of the National Academy of Sciences' National Research Council, and others, we found that views frequently varied on which specific technologies NE should be supporting through its R&D efforts.

High-Temperature Gas-Cooled Reactors

High-temperature gas-cooled reactors produce energy in the form of high-temperature heat—which can produce electricity or be used as process heat—and differ from existing light water reactors in three key features: using (1) helium gas instead of water as a coolant; (2) graphite instead of water to slow neutrons and sustain the nuclear reaction; and (3) advanced nuclear fuel, which offers safety benefits at high temperatures. These three features make high-temperature gas-cooled reactors capable of operating at higher temperatures than existing light water reactors, thus offering a broader range of applications to industrial processes, as well as higher heat-to-electricity energy conversion efficiencies than are achievable with the lower operating temperatures of light water reactors. The high-temperature gas-cooled reactor is an advanced reactor technology that is expected to be helpful in limiting greenhouse gas emissions, according to NE officials, DOE laboratory staff, and NE documents. In addition, the technology offers inherent and passive safety features—including advanced fuel, helium coolant, and passive heat removal—that are especially important in a post-Fukushima world, according to NE officials.

NE's current involvement with high-temperature gas-cooled reactor R&D began in 2002, when, under the Generation-IV International Forum, high-temperature gas-cooled reactor systems were selected as one of six advanced reactor technologies to be developed by the international consortium. The United States was one of six countries, plus the European Union, that took the lead in developing this reactor technology, according to NE officials. NE chose to pursue high-temperature gas-cooled reactors because, according to NE officials, laboratory staff, and NE documents, they met the criteria of its advanced reactor programs, including potential improvements over existing light water reactors in safety, economic viability, and their promise for reducing greenhouse gas emissions. NE officials told us that the high-temperature gas-cooled reactor was also chosen because it had operating history in the United States and throughout the world, which meant that many important technical details had already been resolved. At the time, NE concluded that its research would build on existing operational experience, thus increasing the likelihood that high-temperature gas-cooled reactors could be developed and commercialized. NE envisioned its research would further demonstrate the technical and economic viability of the high-temperature gas-cooled reactor technology.

Pursuant to EPAct 2005, NE is to undertake research, development, design, construction, and operation of an advanced nuclear reactor prototype with a targeted completion date of September 30, 2021.[28] From 2005 to 2011, under Phase 1 of the NGNP Project, NE spent more than $500 million on R&D in support of high-temperature gas-cooled reactor technologies. This research was conducted primarily at DOE's national laboratories, and it focused on preliminary reactor design work, developing new reactor fuel, and testing high-temperature materials. The NGNP Project also collaborates with universities and industry on some R&D activities, and NE has coordinated with NRC to conduct R&D necessary to design and license high-temperature gas-cooled reactors in the United States. The last high-temperature gas-cooled reactor was licensed in the United States in 1973, and many questions remain about the process by which NRC will consider license approval for these reactors. According to NE and NRC officials, NE began consulting with NRC in the mid-2000s as NRC worked to (1) update its policy on the regulation of advanced reactors and (2) produce a report to Congress on its advanced reactor licensing strategy for NGNP, which was jointly published in 2008. During this time, NE shared detailed technical information and supporting materials with NRC, information meant to mitigate risks associated with the licensing process, according to NE and NRC officials. Although DOE determined that it would not proceed to

---

[28]EPAct 2005 also provides that DOE may submit a report to Congress establishing an alternative date for completion.

Phase 2 design activities for the NGNP Project in 2011, NE continues to fund research on some aspects of a high-temperature gas-cooled reactor, including the testing of advanced reactor fuel and high-temperature materials including graphite.

We found varying views on the potential economic feasibility of the high-temperature gas-cooled reactors. Some industry representatives and a member of the National Academy of Sciences' National Research Council that we interviewed questioned the appropriateness of NE continuing to fund high-temperature gas-cooled reactor research, citing concerns over the reactor's economic viability in relation to the current cost of natural gas. One industry representative cited studies showing that the technology is not economically viable, as well as the fact that NE has, to date, been unable to get industrial partners interested in sharing project development costs. However, an economic analysis by the NGNP Industry Alliance—an international consortium of potential end users, owner-operators, and technology companies brought together to partner with NE and commercialize the high-temperature gas-cooled reactor—concluded that the high-temperature gas-cooled reactor would be economically viable under certain market conditions. In addition, NE has conducted a series of feasibility studies, including detailed economic analyses and studies of potential industrial applications for the process heat, to demonstrate conditions under which the high-temperature gas-cooled reactor technology becomes economically competitive. Representatives from the NGNP Industry Alliance said they believe that, with favorable trends in natural gas prices, the high-temperature gas-cooled reactor will be economically viable by the time the prototype reactor is built in the early-2030s, as is projected under the NGNP Industry Alliance's current project time frames.

Liquid-Metal-Cooled Fast Reactors

The liquid-metal-cooled fast reactors, including sodium-cooled fast reactors, use liquid-metal to cool the reactor core. In addition to producing electricity, a primary benefit of these reactors is in nuclear waste management. Fast reactors can use reprocessed spent nuclear fuel as their energy source, which would help the United States reduce the amount of spent fuel from light water reactors that would need to be stored or eventually placed in a geologic repository. Fast reactors also minimize nuclear waste generation by significantly improving fuel use efficiency as compared to traditional light water reactors.

NE identified the sodium-cooled fast reactor as a reactor technology of interest in 2002 under the Generation-IV International Forum because, according to NE officials, it met criteria of its advanced reactor programs, including significant advances in proliferation resistance, its potential for improving the sustainability of the nuclear fuel cycle, and its management of highly radioactive waste elements. NE continues to conduct research in support of sodium-cooled fast reactors because of their advantages for addressing nuclear waste and because reactors with the same basic technology have been built and operated in the United States and around the world since the 1960s. In fact, several other countries, including Japan and France, had or currently have operating sodium-cooled fast reactors.

We also found varying views on sodium-cooled fast reactors among industry representatives, members of the National Academy of Sciences' National Research Council, and others that we interviewed. Some members of the National Academy of Sciences' National Research Council and an industry representative cited concerns over the safety of sodium-cooled fast reactors—including the highly reactive nature of the sodium in the presence of water and the threat of sodium fires—and believe that these safety issues may never be fully overcome. Moreover, some industry representatives and members of the National Academy of Sciences' National Research Council told us that a fast reactor technology market does not exist in the United States, citing other more cost-effective options for storing spent nuclear fuel, including storage in aboveground casks or water pools as is the current practice at U.S. nuclear power reactors. These individuals believe that NE's sodium-cooled fast reactor research is ill-advised.

In contrast, NE officials and some industry representatives that we interviewed believe that remaining technical challenges with the sodium-cooled fast reactor can be overcome. In addition, NE officials said it is conceivable that changes in government policy for handling spent nuclear fuel in the United States will create a market for fast reactors, as it has in the United Kingdom. Moreover, NE believes that the sodium-cooled fast reactor, or other similar fast reactor technology, may be instrumental in efforts to develop a sustainable nuclear fuel cycle. In 2011, NE undertook a comprehensive study of various options for improving the sustainability of the nuclear fuel cycle, which would potentially entail using fast reactor technology and waste reprocessing to create nuclear power systems that better manage and reduce the generation of nuclear waste when compared to a once-through light water reactor fuel cycle. Although this study did not consider specific advanced reactor technologies, a closed fuel cycle may require using an advanced fast reactor technology, such as the sodium-cooled fast reactor.

| Fluoride-Salt-Cooled High-Temperature Reactor | The fluoride-salt-cooled high-temperature reactor design takes advantage of the physical characteristics of liquid-salt coolant to enable the development of a high-temperature system that is scalable to larger power and able to operate at lower pressure and higher power density than the helium-cooled high-temperature gas-cooled reactor. With these characteristics, according to NE officials and DOE documents, these reactors could provide potential safety benefits and increased efficiency over existing light water reactors while maintaining the benefit of providing both electricity and process heat for industrial applications. NE officials told us that this mix of characteristics is the reason why NE provides limited funding research into fluoride-salt-cooled high-temperature reactor. However, the fluoride-salt-cooled high-temperature reactor technology is not very mature or well tested, and because of this is considered more of a long-range advanced reactor technology, according to NE officials. NE funds R&D into fluoride-salt-cooled high-temperature reactors mainly through NE's Nuclear Energy University Program, with the research mainly conducted at universities across the country. Two industry representatives we interviewed took issue with NE for funding a reactor technology that is unproven and that in their view has little chance of ever being built. In response, NE officials told us that the potential benefits of fluoride-salt-cooled high-temperature reactor over other advanced reactor technologies warrant providing limited funds and utilizing university research capabilities. |

Other Advanced Nuclear Reactor Technologies

NE conducts or funds R&D on other advanced reactor technologies on a small scale, mainly to assess their potential and better characterize their performance capabilities. NE officials told us that most of these technologies have some unproven aspects, operate in novel ways, or have other characteristics that increase the risk associated with their development. NE supports research into some of these potentially transformative, long-term technology options through its Nuclear Energy University Program. For example, in 2013, the program funded research to assess the feasibility of an advanced reactor fueled with depleted uranium, a design offering a 30-fold increase in uranium ore utilization verses contemporary light water reactor designs.

NE also funds research into promising advanced reactor technologies through the Advanced Reactor Concepts Technical Review Panel process. Through this process, NE identifies R&D needs for potentially viable advanced reactor technologies to inform NE advanced reactor R&D funding decisions. A goal of the process is to facilitate greater engagement between DOE and the nuclear industry. NE first solicited information on advanced reactor proposals from industry in February

2012, after which a review panel made up of experts from national laboratories, universities, and industry reviewed the proposals against established evaluation criteria, including safety, market attractiveness, economics, proliferation risk, waste generation, security, and potential regulatory challenges. The panel's assessment of market attractiveness focused on the proposed technologies' ability to be competitive in the marketplace, and it included variables like efficiency, initial capital costs, and economic factors such as construction, manufacturing, and operating costs and uncertainties, as well as the resulting cost of electricity, according to the Technical Review Panel report. The objective of the Technical Review Panel process was to evaluate the viability of the technologies, understand the R&D needs of each, and prioritize research to support development and commercialization of each. After R&D needs and priorities were identified, NE issued a funding opportunity announcement, competitively selected four projects, and provided a total of $3.5 million in funding for those projects, according to NE officials. Many nuclear industry representatives we interviewed applauded NE's effort and told us that this process was an effective way for NE to collaborate with industry and that it begins to address a long-standing industry concern that NE's R&D efforts did not coordinate with industry or meet industry needs. However, these industry representatives also stated that the $3.5 million in R&D funding was insufficient to meaningfully address the need for collaboration between NE and industry as it was enough to fund a very small number of R&D activities. Notably, Congress provided NE with an additional $12 million to support a continuation of this effort. According to NE officials, NE has issued another industry solicitation and will use the information gathered to make additional industry cost-shared R&D awards early in fiscal year 2015.

Advanced Small Modular Reactors

NE also conducts research on advanced small modular reactors with the goal of supporting the development of innovative small modular reactor designs that offer improved safety, functionality, and affordability. These R&D efforts support advanced small modular reactors that offer simplified operation and maintenance, more efficient energy conversion, and increased proliferation resistance and security. More specifically, NE funds research on advanced sensors, instrumentation and controls, control systems for multiple units, advanced materials, and other major system components. In addition, NE funds efforts to create standards and codes for small modular reactor materials to support the eventual licensing of these advanced reactor technologies.

In 2012 and 2013, through its Small Modular Reactor Licensing Technical Support program, NE issued funding opportunity announcements for cost-sharing with industry for the development of small modular reactor designs—including small modular reactors based on light water reactor technology, as well as advanced small modular reactors—to support the program's vision to provide additional nuclear power options that offer more flexibility in financing, siting, and end-use applications than large light water reactor designs. Under the cost-sharing arrangement for each funding opportunity, DOE is supporting design development, first-of-a-kind engineering, experiments, and analysis in support of gaining design certification approval from NRC for the small modular reactors so that commercial deployment of the first small modular reactor can begin. Industry proposals under these announcements were judged by independent selection panels based on a series of criteria, including the extent to which the design incorporates safety, operability, efficiency, economics, and security characteristics that exceed the capabilities of current reactor designs; the likelihood of expeditiously achieving design certification and deployment;[29] the overall quality of the project plan and business approach; and other factors. Based on our review of the two funding opportunity announcements, however, we found that the funding opportunity announcements differed in the economic information that NE required for proposals. In the 2012 announcement, NE more directly addressed economics and marketability by requiring applicants to propose business plans "to meet expanding domestic electricity requirements at a competitive price" and to "provide their plan to achieve successful commercial deployment" of the technology. By contrast, the 2013 announcement indicated that the economic criteria used to evaluate proposals would be based on the designs' construction, fabrication, deployment, and operational costs. NE officials told us that these criteria indirectly assess economics and marketability of these technologies, and that the type of economic information received from applicants in 2012 was very preliminary and did not provide a good discriminator with which to evaluate proposals. In addition, these officials stated that it was incumbent on the applicants to ultimately assure marketability as they were providing most of the funding and have a profit motive. For both funding opportunity announcements, the panel's evaluation resulted in choosing a small modular reactor design based on conventional light water reactor technology. Some industry representatives, members of the National Academy of Sciences' National Research Council and the

---

[29]The March 2012 funding opportunity announcement had a target date of 2022 for deployment. The March 2013 funding opportunity announcement had a target date of 2025 for deployment.

Nuclear Energy Advisory Committee, and NE officials told us that this selection was an appropriate choice because it has a significantly better chance of being licensed and constructed in the required time frame, as compared to advanced small modular reactor designs that are not based on conventional light water reactor technology.

NE's Approach Addresses Broad Programmatic Goals and Policy Objectives, and Provides Flexibility in Responding to Changes in U.S. Energy Policy

While the broad goals of NE's advanced reactor R&D efforts are to improve the economics, safety, and proliferation resistance of nuclear power plants, the R&D efforts also aim to develop advanced reactor technologies that can prepare the United States to address policy objectives such as reducing nuclear waste and greenhouse gas emissions. NE's approach to advanced reactor R&D is to conduct research in support of multiple advanced reactor technologies. According to NE officials and documents, because NE's approach to advanced reactor R&D has multiple goals and seeks to address several different policy objectives, NE works on multiple technologies simultaneously. A key objective of NE's advanced reactor R&D efforts is to conduct research to remove technology barriers or reduce technology risks, while collaborating with industry and academia, with the ultimate goal for industry to take the results of NE's research to the next step of development and commercialization. NE focuses on R&D that industry does not have the means to carry out, according to NE officials, with the expectation that the research will reduce financial risks to industry and thereby increase the affordability of industry investment in new nuclear technologies. In addition, NE engages and collaborates with NRC on issues related to the eventual licensing of advanced reactors, including understanding the likely scope and extent of R&D necessary to support the licensing process.

While advanced reactors are attractive for many reasons, NE carries out research on a variety of reactors because, in part, different reactor types can address particular objectives, according to NE officials. For instance, fast reactors can be better at addressing the nuclear waste issue than some other advanced reactors, while high-temperature gas-cooled reactors provide process heat and may be a better solution for addressing greenhouse gas emissions. According to NE officials, the development of fast reactors, such as the sodium-cooled fast reactor, is likely to play a critical role in managing spent nuclear fuel if and when the United States decides to reprocess and use its spent nuclear fuel rather than store it at reactor sites,[30] as is the current practice at U.S. nuclear power reactors, or isolate it in a geologic repository underground, as has been proposed.[31]

To remain aware of industry's R&D needs and international nuclear energy developments, NE regularly collaborates with industry and international organizations, according to NE officials and NE documents. NE officials told us that NE regularly collaborates with industry on specific R&D projects by sharing technical data and information. For example, NE is currently collaborating with industry on advanced fuels and materials, among other things. NE officials told us they work with industry and have conversations regarding specific R&D activities. According to NE officials and some industry representatives that we interviewed, this type of collaboration has been increasing in recent years, and one industry representative stated that such collaboration is critically important to ensuring that NE's activities are relevant for industry.

One way that NE has recently collaborated with industry, according to NE officials, was through the Advanced Reactor Concepts Technical Review Panel process. Some industry representatives we talked to stated that this review panel process was beneficial to both industry and NE because it helped inform NE of industry R&D needs and because it has provided some funds to industry to carry out research on promising new technologies. Industry officials also told us that the process has opened up some new channels of communication between NE and industry. However, industry representatives also stated that, although this collaboration with industry is beneficial, NE could be doing more to ensure that its R&D is more fully aligned with industry needs. For

---

[30]Spent nuclear fuel can no longer efficiently generate power in a nuclear reactor, but it can be reprocessed to separate out uranium and plutonium which may be used again to fuel a reactor. Reprocessing, however, results in nuclear waste that requires disposal. The United States does not currently reprocess its spent nuclear fuel, and this fuel, when it is accepted for disposal, is considered to be high-level waste as defined by NRC.

[31]The Nuclear Waste Policy Act of 1982 directed DOE to investigate sites for a federal geologic repository to dispose of spent nuclear fuel and high-level nuclear waste from commercial nuclear power plants. In 1986, DOE recommended three candidate sites for characterization, but in 1987, the Nuclear Waste Policy Amendments Act of 1987 directed DOE to focus its efforts only on Yucca Mountain, a site about 100 miles northwest of Las Vegas, Nevada. In March 2009, the Secretary of Energy announced plans to terminate the Yucca Mountain repository program. See GAO-12-797 for more information. The administration's current strategy proposes to move spent fuel from reactor sites to an interim storage facility for eventual disposal in a geological repository underground.

example, according to one industry official, NE conducts some research that, while interesting and potentially beneficial, has little utility for industry's current needs.

NE carries out international collaboration through ongoing meetings of the Generation-IV International Forum and through the International Atomic Energy Agency,[32] through the Organisation for Economic Co-operation and Development (OECD),[33] and through bi-lateral agreements with many countries around the world, including Canada, the Russian Federation, the People's Republic of China, Japan, the Republic of Korea, and countries in the European Union. NE officials cited several examples of such collaboration, such as with the People's Republic of China on high-temperature gas-cooled reactors; with France on their sodium-cooled fast reactor development project; with Japan on advanced materials for sodium-cooled fast reactors; and with the Republic of Korea on sodium-cooled fast reactors.

NE's approach to advanced reactor R&D provides several advantages, primarily flexibility in responding to changes in future U.S. energy policy or other circumstances, according to NE officials. The officials said they believe that conducting research in support of multiple advanced reactor technologies gives the agency the flexibility to respond to external factors affecting the direction of their advanced reactor R&D efforts, including changes in U.S. energy policy, energy markets, or other areas. Specifically, NE officials told us that the current approach positions NE to respond to changes in U.S. energy policies, such as policies for managing the nation's nuclear waste or controlling greenhouse gas emissions. Changes in either of these policies would affect the direction of NE's advanced reactor efforts, according to NE officials. For instance, a policy calling for the United States to manage nuclear waste by reprocessing spent nuclear fuel and reusing it as reactor fuel would result

---

[32]The International Atomic Energy Agency is an autonomous international organization affiliated with the United Nations, established in Vienna, Austria, in 1957. The agency has the dual role of promoting the peaceful uses of nuclear energy by transferring nuclear science and technology through its nuclear science and applications and technical cooperation programs, and verifying, through its safeguards program, that nuclear material subject to safeguards is not diverted to nuclear weapons or other proscribed purposes.

[33]The OECD is an organization of 34 industrialized countries, operating by consensus, that fosters dialogue among members to discuss, develop, and refine economic and social policies and provides an arena for establishing multilateral agreements.

in NE focusing efforts and concentrating resources on developing and deploying fast reactor technologies. NE officials told us that the current practice of storing nuclear waste in aboveground facilities at nuclear power plants across the country will eventually be changed, and waste will either be moved to long-term underground repositories, or reprocessed and burned in fast nuclear reactors.[34] NE officials told us that ongoing research into fast reactor technologies is important so that NE is positioned to react to changes in U.S. policy toward the handling of nuclear waste, including waste that has already been generated and waste that continues to be generated.

Similarly, NE officials said that policies that affect the prices of various energy sources would have an effect on the commercial attractiveness of high-temperature reactors, including high-temperature gas-cooled reactors. For instance, officials cited the possibility of the imposition of a carbon tax to control greenhouse gas emissions, or the possibility of natural gas prices rising, either of which would make nuclear energy more economically competitive and increase the attractiveness of the high-temperature gas-cooled reactors that produce both electricity and process heat for industrial applications. These industrial applications currently rely heavily on natural gas or coal plants as their source for high-temperature process heat. NE officials stated that natural gas prices in other countries are already at levels where the high-temperature gas-cooled reactors are projected to be economically competitive and that this has resulted in some interest from outside the United States in the development of this technology.

According to NE officials, another advantage of NE's approach to advanced reactor R&D is that NE is able to maintain an employee base with knowledge and expertise on a wide variety of reactor technologies. NE officials told us that maintaining staff expertise is important so NE can continue to conduct research on the various technologies, train the next generation of scientists and engineers, and be ready to support the production of prototype reactors when the time comes. In addition, maintaining a level of expertise in a variety of advanced reactor technologies means that NE can engage with, monitor, and support other

---

[34]Current reprocessing techniques, aimed at extracting usable uranium and plutonium from spent fuel, have been developed for use in light water reactors. However, spent fuel from light water reactors contains other radioactive isotopes that a fast reactor can eliminate from the waste stream.

countries as they develop advanced reactor technologies. These officials said this is important because other countries are actively developing advanced reactor technologies, and the United States needs scientists that can understand how those reactors operate, in part, to judge their safety and nuclear proliferation risks.

NE officials also said that conducing R&D on several types of advanced reactors simultaneously, rather than focusing on a single reactor type, also gives NE the ability to fund R&D supporting promising but unproven reactor technologies. For instance, NE is funding limited research on lead-cooled fast reactors, which offer the potential for improved safety and proliferation resistance over other advanced reactor technologies, but they have some unproven technologies and components, according to NE officials. Similarly, NE is funding research in support of an advanced small modular reactor based on fast reactor technology that would potentially address the nuclear waste issue and also provide process heat for industrial applications. NE officials said that it is important to have funds available to support these and other potentially game-changing technological breakthroughs. However, in its June 2013 report, the Nuclear Energy Advisory Committee was critical of NE's approach, saying that NE needs to better prioritize its R&D efforts on a smaller number of advanced reactor technologies to focus research funding on the ultimate goal of deploying an advanced reactor prototype.

Although NE selected the technology to develop under the NGNP Project, many members of the National Academy of Sciences' National Research Council, members of the Nuclear Energy Advisory Committee, and industry representatives we interviewed agree with NE's approach to advanced reactor R&D because the time is not right for NE to move to the deployment phase. For instance, representatives from industry and the Nuclear Energy Advisory Committee told us that uncertainties around current policies for handing nuclear waste and controlling greenhouse gases do not make a compelling case for choosing an advanced reactor technology to deploy as a prototype. The 2008 National Academy of Sciences' National Research Council review of NE's advanced reactor R&D efforts agreed with NE's approach to advanced reactor R&D, saying that there are several policy matters and other questions—undetermined nuclear waste management options, unformulated environmental policy, ongoing work of other countries on advanced technologies, and unclear nonproliferation regimes—that will affect NE's decisions and priorities. This review team stated that, given these unknowns, it would be premature to select a winning technology from among current options.

In addition, in January 2012, the President's Blue Ribbon Commission on America's Nuclear Future recommended having the United States continue multiple near-term (i.e., light water reactor) and long-term (e.g., small modular reactor, sodium-cooled fast reactor, high-temperature gas-cooled reactor) R&D efforts until NE could defensibly select technologies that would meet certain regulatory and policy requirements (e.g., safety, environmental protection, security, and nonproliferation). Moreover, members of the Nuclear Energy Advisory Committee and the National Academy of Sciences' National Research Council, and representatives from industry told us that current NE funding levels would prohibit NE from deploying a prototype reactor even if NE chose an advanced technology to deploy. Some of them said that NE is correctly positioning itself to be prepared to deploy a prototype reactor in the long-term as policies or energy markets change. One Nuclear Energy Advisory Committee representative said that United States could focus its advanced reactor R&D efforts quickly in response to a policy change or other congressional direction, provided that NE also saw increased funding.

NE Uses Internal and External Reviews to Set Program and Funding Priorities but Does Not Have a Strategy for Deploying an Advanced Reactor Prototype

NE's uses internal and external reviews to set program and funding priorities for advanced reactor R&D and to evaluate progress toward program goals. However, NE does not have a strategy for overcoming barriers to deploying an advanced nuclear reactor prototype, increasing the likelihood that such a reactor will not be built by the 2021 target date specified in EPAct 2005. Not deploying a prototype carries certain risks, including waning U.S. influence in the safe operation of nuclear plants internationally and potential loss of certain knowledge and expertise.

NE Plans, Prioritizes, and Evaluates Its R&D Activities through Internal and External Reviews

NE takes a number of steps to plan and prioritize its advanced reactor R&D efforts and evaluate progress toward program goals. Before its annual program planning meetings, NE and national laboratory staff develop a list of R&D efforts considered to be priorities. NE management reviews this information in light of program goals, including long-term goals described in NE's 2010 R&D Roadmap, program funding, and schedules, according to NE officials. Once the research priorities are established and approved by management, the individual laboratories develop detailed work plans, which describe the objectives and scope of the work to be performed. These work plans are reviewed to ensure that the proposed work is aligned with NE's mission and that the work can be accomplished within the allotted budget and time frames, according to NE officials. All of the approved work plans are then entered into NE's performance management system—the Program Information Collection System—which allows NE to track progress toward budget and schedule milestones on an ongoing basis. According to a laboratory staff member, this system tracks progress toward short-term goals—on a monthly basis—and long-term goals—on yearly, 3-year, and 5-year time frames.

NE monitors and evaluates its advanced reactor R&D activities on an ongoing basis through the Program Information Collection System and conducts program reviews—monthly, quarterly, and annually—to assess progress toward program goals, according to NE officials. For example, officials from the Advanced Reactor Concepts and Advanced Small Modular Reactor subprograms hold monthly progress review meetings to discuss, among other things, program updates, technical highlights, and budget and milestone status updates. The officials use monthly status tracking reports generated by the performance management system as part of these reviews, in which officials review cost and schedule performance data. In addition to the monthly meetings, officials from the Advanced Reactor Concepts and Advanced Small Modular Reactor subprograms typically conduct four in-depth reviews of each year, according to NE officials. These reviews focus on one or more specific areas of research, and officials discuss progress toward goals, important issues or problems, and plans going forward. For example, the meeting minutes from the quarterly review of the Advanced Reactor Concepts and Advanced Small Modular Reactor subprograms in July 2013 show that officials discussed accomplishments and also priorities for the upcoming fiscal year, and conducted in-depth discussions of certain program areas and overviews of others. In addition, NE conducts annual reviews of activities across multiple subprograms and topics to ensure that NE's efforts are complementary and nonduplicative, and also to gain insight into areas of potential collaboration. For example, during its annual review of the nuclear reactor R&D efforts in March 2014, NE officials discussed progress on fuels for the high-temperature gas-cooled reactor, advanced reactor licensing, and advanced reactor materials for small modular reactors, among other things. On a less-formal basis, management officials at the national laboratories are in frequent communication with NE management through weekly teleconferences to provide regular progress updates and provide information on unforeseen circumstances or challenges, according to NE officials.

NE also takes steps to coordinate efforts across its R&D programs and subprograms to leverage experience and funding, as well as to reduce redundant R&D activities. Officials from the Advanced Reactor Concepts and Fuel Cycle subprograms stated that they frequently coordinate with each other because their R&D efforts are interdependent. For example, the Fuel Cycle subprogram is conducting R&D on accident tolerant fuels that will be used for advanced reactors, so coordination between the Fuel Cycle subprogram and the Advanced Reactor Concepts subprogram is crucial, according to NE officials.

To further help ensure that R&D efforts are coordinated and to minimize redundancies, NE established the Nuclear Energy Enabling Technologies program in fiscal year 2011. The program is designed to conduct R&D on crosscutting technologies that complement NE's activities to support and enable the development of new advanced reactor designs and fuel cycle technologies. NE created the program to better coordinate and integrate R&D activities after officials identified some similar efforts being performed on crosscutting areas, such as materials, across more than one program, according to NE officials. Through this program, NE has awarded over $9 million to support R&D projects focused on reactor materials, advanced sensors and instrumentation, and advanced methods for manufacturing, among other things. NE determines which R&D efforts are conducted by the Nuclear Energy Enabling Technologies program by reviewing R&D proposals submitted by different groups, including the national labs, universities, research institutions, and industry, according to NE documents. Specific R&D projects are selected based on common needs of programs and subprograms, with each selected project required to support at least three programs or subprograms.

Others also periodically conduct external reviews of NE's advanced reactor R&D to inform the planning and prioritization efforts for and assess the progress of its R&D activities. Most prominently, according to NE officials, the Nuclear Energy Advisory Committee provides NE with independent advice and recommendations on complex science and technical issues that arise in planning, managing, and implementing NE's R&D activities. The Nuclear Energy Advisory Committee typically meets twice annually with NE management to discuss its reports and recommendations. The Nuclear Energy Advisory Committee's subcommittee on Nuclear Reactor Technology is intended to provide expert guidance to NE on both the short-term and long-term direction of its R&D efforts on reactor technologies. NE officials and Nuclear Energy Advisory Committee representatives told us that the committee has been beneficial in providing expertise to NE and that NE has been responsive to the committee's recommendations. In 2011, a Nuclear Energy Advisory Committee review of NE's R&D efforts on the NGNP Project determined that NE should not move forward with the complete set of Phase 2 activities of the project, citing constraints imposed by EPAct 2005 and difficulties finding industry partners. Subsequently, in 2011, NE informed Congress that it would not proceed with Phase 2 design activities of the NGNP Project until circumstances warranted a change in direction.

NE's efforts have also been reviewed by other outside entities, including the Secretary of Energy's Advisory Board, which provides advice and recommendations to the Secretary of Energy on various topics. For example, in 2012, the Secretary of Energy requested the board identify areas in which standards for safety, security, and nonproliferation should be developed for small modular reactors; identify challenges, uncertainties, and risks to commercialization; and provide advice on approaches to manage these risks and accelerate deployment of these reactors. The board determined that the commercialization of small modular reactors was likely to produce multiple benefits for the country, including helping provide for a more reliable power grid with more widely distributed power generation once current light water reactors are retired; supporting clean generation and reduced carbon emissions; and helping preserve influence of the United States on nuclear nonproliferation issues. The board stated that to deploy small modular reactors widely, the nation must develop a robust small modular reactor industry that can manufacture cost-competitive small modular reactors that meet U.S. regulatory standards, and that the primary risk for commercialization of these reactors, beyond design certification and licensing, is the ability to drive the plant costs down sufficiently to become competitive with other energy sources, such as natural gas, without compromising safety and security. To develop this industry, according to the board, the U.S. government will likely have to play a significant financial role beyond the Small Modular Reactor Licensing Technical Support program.

NE Does Not Have a Strategy to Overcome Several Barriers to Deploying an Advanced Nuclear Reactor Prototype

Although NE's primary mission is to advance nuclear power through research, development, and demonstration, its deployment of an advanced reactor prototype under the NGNP Project is unlikely in the foreseeable future. Among the different advanced reactor technologies currently supported by NE R&D, the high-temperature gas-cooled reactor technology is the most likely to be deployed and commercialized in the near term, according to an NE planning document. NE officials said that the likelihood is based on the wide range of potential market applications to industry of electricity and process heat and is supported by substantial government investments in the technology's development, including testing of materials, fuels, and other components. NE has consulted with the NGNP Industry Alliance on the project, including discussing the alliance's plan for proceeding with development of a prototype reactor. In addition, NE has done market research on potential industrial applications for the process heat. Further, NE established a contract in 2013 with NGNP Industry Alliance to develop economic analyses detailing how industry may best engage in developing and commercializing high-temperature gas-cooled reactor technologies. According to laboratory staff, development and testing of the advanced fuel for high-temperature gas-cooled reactor has progressed positively, and other research on high-temperature materials and other components has produced positive results.[35]

In 2011, DOE informed Congress that it would not proceed with Phase 2 design activities for the NGNP Project until circumstances warranted a change in direction. According to NE officials, laboratory staff, and representatives of the NGNP Industry Alliance, the NGNP Project remains hindered by several barriers. Specifically, barriers are as follows:

- **Cost-share requirements.** DOE's attempts to implement the cost-share provisions in EPAct 2005 for the NGNP Projects have met with resistance from industry, according to DOE officials and industry representatives, because of differences in how EPAct 2005 is interpreted by NE and by the NGNP Industry Alliance. EPAct 2005 provides that activities by industry must be cost-shared in accordance with the research, development, demonstration, and commercial application cost-sharing provisions established under section 988 of the act. Specifically, the Secretary must require cost-sharing in accordance with this cost-sharing provision when carrying out a research, development, demonstration, or commercial application program or activity that is initiated after August 8, 2005. For applied

---

[35]As discussed above, some advanced reactor technologies have more significant technical and economic barriers to overcome, and thus are not realistic candidates for deployment in the near term. For instance, while NE could prioritize the sodium-cooled fast reactor, some industry representatives and members of the National Academy of Sciences' National Research Council told us that a fast reactor technology market does not exist in the United States. Other advanced reactors, such as fluoride salt-cooled high-temperature reactors and lead-cooled fast reactors, are not very mature or well tested, or have unproven technologies and components, according to NE officials.

research and development activities, industry generally is to provide not less than 20 percent of the cost, but the cost-share may be reduced or eliminated if the Secretary determines doing so is necessary and appropriate. For demonstration and commercial application activities, industry generally is to provide not less than 50 percent of the cost, but the cost-share may be reduced if the Secretary determines that doing so is necessary and appropriate considering any technological risk relating to the activity. However, according to NE officials and representatives from the NGNP Industry Alliance, they have been unable to come to an agreement on implementing the cost-share requirement for funding the remainder of the NGNP Project because of disagreement on the applicable cost-share levels and how and when the cost-share would be applied to specific activities or project phases. The NGNP Industry Alliance favors meeting the total cost-share requirement by measuring costs over the course of the remainder of the NGNP Project rather than on an annual basis. According to the NGNP Industry Alliance cost-share proposal from November 2009, the alliance suggested assessing a lower industry cost-share in the first years of the project and increasing the industry share over time, with industry paying the vast share of the annual project costs by the final years of the project. Under this proposed scenario, the alliance states that the cumulative industry contribution would meet the overall cost-share requirement, and NE's portion of the development costs would largely be paid up front. DOE did not fully consider the alliance's proposal for a multiyear approach to the cost-share requirement, according to NE officials, because the project was not proceeding at the time due to funding constraints, competing program priorities, and other factors

Representatives from the NGNP Industry Alliance told us that cost-sharing the development activities on a annual basis is not feasible because it would mean a substantial layout of funds with a very long payoff time and would expose the industry partners to significant financial risks. NGNP Industry Alliance representatives said these risks include unknowns associated with obtaining regulatory approval from NRC for the prototype reactor, and the risk that NE will not be provided sufficient funds through congressional appropriations to meet its obligations. NE officials told us that they understand the NGNP Industry Alliance's perspective and had been attempting to work out an agreement when DOE decided not to proceed to Phase 2 of the project. Representatives from the NGNP Industry Alliance told us that the impasse over cost-sharing needs to be resolved in order to proceed with the NGNP advanced reactor prototype.

- **Site requirement.** According to NE officials, laboratory staff, and NGNP Industry Alliance representatives, the EPAct 2005 requirement that the NGNP reactor prototype be located at the Idaho National Laboratory is another barrier to proceeding with the project. Representatives of the NGNP Industry Alliance said that part of the economic benefit of the reactor prototype would be the use of the high-temperature process heat that results from operating the high-temperature gas-cooled reactor. Alliance representatives said that building the reactor at Idaho National Laboratory foregoes the economic benefit because industries that could potentially use process heat are not located near the laboratory, making the overall prototype reactor less economically attractive. Instead, they told us that the NGNP prototype reactor should be located where the petrochemical or other industries that use process heat could benefit from it. This is consistent with a finding in the Nuclear Energy Advisory Committee's 2011 Phase 1 review of the NGNP Project. In its review, the committee stated that the business case to optimize NGNP use for process heat applications and electricity indicates that a site in proximity to a wide range of industrial uses is more appropriate and that a siting at the Idaho National Laboratory will not support a partnership agreement with industry. If industry cannot realize an economic benefit from the prototype reactor, it is unlikely that industry would support the reactor being built at the Idaho National Laboratory.
- **Fiscal constraints and competing priorities.** NE officials, laboratory staff, industry representatives, and Nuclear Energy Advisory Committee members that we interviewed told us that NE's recent funding levels are inadequate to move forward with the NGNP prototype reactor. NE officials and the NGNP Industry Alliance both estimate that NE's share of NGNP Project could amount to as much as $2 billion over the remainder of the project, in which costs would be shared with industry. Under the NGNP Industry Alliance's proposal, DOE would provide between approximately $170 million and $330 million annually over the first 6 years of the proposed plan. This compares to the total funding for Advanced Reactor Concepts subprogram of about $60 million in 2014. NE officials, Nuclear Energy Advisory Committee members, and laboratory staff told us that NE's funding levels are inadequate to move forward toward a prototype reactor, even if it were to focus its resources on one effort. Furthermore, an NE officials and a member of the Nuclear Energy Advisory Committee told us that current priorities to fund R&D aimed at sustaining the existing light water reactors and focusing on the design and licensing of small modular reactors would have to shift in order to make more funds available for advanced reactor R&D.

- **Competition from natural gas.** NE officials, some industry representatives, and Nuclear Energy Advisory Committee members that we interviewed told us that low natural gas prices have made nuclear energy less attractive economically over the past few years, reducing overall interest in nuclear power options. NE officials and industry representatives said that the current atmosphere is not conducive to partnering with industry on advanced reactor projects, including the NGNP Project.

The Secretary's October 2011 letter to Congress did not specify which conditions might warrant a change in program direction—that is, proceed with Phase 2 of the NGNP Project—and NE has not developed a strategy for overcoming the identified barriers hindering the resumption of the project or a set of criteria for determining when a change in program direction would occur. An NE management official that we interviewed stated that conditions that would warrant a change in direction might include Congress legislating a carbon tax, a rise in price of natural gas, or an increase in funding for the NGNP. In addition, developing such a strategy may involve consultation with the Nuclear Energy Advisory Committee and others, including independent nuclear experts. Without a strategy for overcoming the barriers hindering the restart of the NGNP Project and identifying conditions NE can use for determining when a change in program direction would occur, it will be difficult for NE to demonstrate that it is poised to move forward, and it risks the project being on hold indefinitely.

According to EPAct 2005, NE was required to select the initial reactor design parameters to be used for the NGNP Project by September 30, 2011, or submit a report to Congress establishing an alternative date for making the selection. However, the Secretary's 2011 letter to Congress did not specify initial design parameters for the NGNP or specify an alternative date for making a selection. Instead, the letter stated that the initial design parameters had not yet been selected and that such a selection would be made by the public-private partnership once it is formed. Without selecting initial reactor design parameters or establishing a date to make a selection as required by EPAct 2005, it is not clear if or when NE is going to take this next step in deploying the NGNP prototype reactor.

In addition, after the Secretary's decision not to proceed with Phase 2 design activities, NE's engagement with NRC on licensing issues has decreased. NE maintains a team seeking to engage NRC on NGNP licensing issues, according to NE officials, but NRC has reassigned staff from its NGNP work and engages with NE on a minimal basis, according to NRC officials. NRC officials said that they cannot proceed substantively further in developing a licensing framework until NE has developed a specific design for an advanced reactor technology.

Furthermore, not deploying an advanced reactor prototype carries some risks, according to some industry representatives, Nuclear Energy Advisory Committee members, and NE officials we interviewed. Specifically, these risks include (1) falling behind other countries in advanced reactor development and losing market share in the global market for nuclear energy; (2) losing influence on which reactor technologies are developed, which raises safety and nuclear proliferation concerns; and (3) losing its ability to manufacture the components necessary to construct nuclear plants.

By not deploying an advanced reactor prototype, the United States risks falling behind other countries—such as Japan, Russia, China, South Korea, and France—that are actively working to deploy and commercialize advanced reactors, according to a Nuclear Energy Advisory Committee report. For example, Russia currently has two sodium-cooled fast reactors—one experimental and one commercial—in operation and is developing or constructing additional sodium-cooled fast reactor technologies, and it has plans to export reactor technology to other nations. In addition, China has an operating sodium-cooled fast reactor and high-temperature gas-cooled reactor on a test reactor scale and is in the process of building a prototype high temperature gas-cooled reactor, according to NE officials. In potentially losing its global leadership position in developing nuclear technologies, the United States risks losing market share in the global market for nuclear energy, which would cost the U.S. economy high-paying jobs in the nuclear industry, according to these individuals.

By falling behind other countries in advanced reactor development, the United States also risks losing influence on determinations of which reactor technologies are developed, with implications for the safety of reactor operations worldwide, as well as implications for how resistant the technologies are to nuclear proliferation—including the safe, effective disposal of nuclear waste—according to NE officials, laboratory staff, and Nuclear Energy Advisory Committee members that we spoke to. Specifically, according to members of the Nuclear Energy Advisory Committee, if the nation is not leading the development of advanced reactors, other countries may operate reactors that do not meet the highest safety standards and may not take adequate steps to ensure nuclear waste is handled appropriately and properly secured.

Similarly, the United States risks losing its ability to manufacture the components necessary to construct nuclear plants, according laboratory staff and Nuclear Energy Advisory Committee members that we interviewed. In addition, by not deploying an advanced reactor, NE risks losing staff, including engineers with the knowledge and experience necessary to design and build advanced reactors, according to an NE official and laboratory staff. For example, without a specific goal of developing an advanced reactor prototype, NE staff are more likely to leave NE for jobs with a better sense of mission, according to these officials.

Conclusions

Energy demand in the United States is expected to rise considerably over the coming decades, and concerns remain over energy security and greenhouse gas emissions from the burning of fossil fuels. While nuclear energy accounts for about 20 percent of electricity generation in the United States and produces no air pollution or greenhouse gases, the accident at Japan's Fukushima Daiichi commercial nuclear power plant in March 2011 highlighted ongoing concerns about the safety of nuclear plants, and concerns also exist about potential threats of nuclear proliferation and terrorism. With this in mind, it is important that nuclear power plants continue to evolve and provide energy economically, while also addressing safety and proliferation concerns. By conducting nuclear reactor R&D, NE has a critical role to play as it supports existing light water reactors, as well as a new generation of advanced nuclear reactors.

However, in 2011, DOE informed Congress that it would not proceed with Phase 2 of the NGNP Project until circumstances warranted a change in direction, and the project remains hindered by several barriers, including the cost-share and site requirements of EPAct 2005. NE officials have attempted to work out a cost-share agreement with the alliance, but different interpretations of the cost-share requirements by DOE and the NGNP Industry Alliance have created an impasse, and no agreement had been reached before DOE determined that it would not proceed to Phase 2 of the project.

Another barrier to proceeding with the project is the EPAct 2005 requirement that the NGNP reactor prototype be located at the Idaho National Laboratory. Building the reactor there foregoes the economic benefit of the reactor's process heat because industries that could potentially use the prototype reactor's high-temperature process heat are not located near the laboratory. If industry cannot realize an economic benefit from the prototype reactor, it is unlikely that industry would support the reactor being built at the Idaho National Laboratory.

Moreover, DOE's October 2011 letter notified Congress that the department had selected the NGNP technology, as required by EPAct 2005, acknowledged that the department had not selected the initial design parameters for the NGNP or identified the date upon which it would do so by September 30, 2011, as required by EPAct 2005, and essentially put Phase 2 of the NGNP Project on hold until conditions favorable to completing the NGNP warranted a change in direction. However, the letter did not specify which conditions might warrant a change in program direction—that is, proceed with Phase 2 of the NGNP Project—and NE has not developed a strategy for overcoming the identified barriers hindering restarting the project or which contains such conditions. Without a strategy for overcoming the barriers hindering the restart of the NGNP Project and identifying conditions NE can use for determining when a change in program direction would occur, the project may be on hold indefinitely. Furthermore, without selecting initial reactor design parameters and reporting the parameters to Congress, as required by EPAct 2005 for completing Phase 1 of the project, or establishing a date to make a selection, it is not clear if or when NE is going to take this next step and proceed with Phase 2 of the NGNP Project.

Recommendations for Executive Action

To better prepare the Department of Energy to meet the requirement of the Energy Policy Act of 2005 to deploy the NGNP prototype reactor, we recommend that DOE take the following two actions:

- Develop, in consultation with the Nuclear Energy Advisory Committee and independent nuclear experts, as appropriate, a strategy to proceed with Phase 2 of the NGNP Project, outlining conditions that will warrant a change in program direction, remaining research and development activities, projected project budget and schedule, and steps necessary to overcome barriers to successful completion of the NGNP Project.
- Provide a report to Congress complying with the statutory requirement for Phase 1 of the NGNP Project by providing initial design parameters or a date for providing them. The report should also provide an updated status of the issues DOE identified in its 2011 letter to Congress and outline any additional barriers to proceeding with Phase 2 of the project, including

- the status of the establishment of a public-private partnership;
- the project strategy, including conditions that would warrant restarting the project; and
- a legislative proposal, if necessary, to address any barriers to proceeding with the project, including the site and cost-share requirements.

Agency Comments and Our Evaluation

We provided a draft of this report to DOE for review and comment. In written comments, DOE's Assistant Secretary for Nuclear Energy, responding on behalf of DOE, wrote that DOE agreed in principle with our first recommendation and respectfully disagreed with our second recommendation. DOE's written comments on our draft report are reproduced in appendix II. In addition, DOE provided technical comments, which we incorporated in the report as appropriate.

In its comment letter, DOE stated that it agreed in principle with our recommendation that it develop a strategy to proceed with Phase 2 of the NGNP Project. Moreover, DOE stated that its current strategy is to continue updating analyses of requirements for successful commercialization of reactor technology to reflect changing market conditions, research and development accomplishments, and the maturity of the licensing framework. However, this strategy does not outline steps DOE could take to proactively overcome the barriers hindering the resumption of the NGNP Project, nor does it outline criteria for determining when a change in program direction would occur. We continue to believe that developing a strategy to proceed with Phase 2 of the NGNP Project is important because without a strategy it will be difficult for NE to demonstrate that, upon completion of Phase 1, it will be poised to develop a final design and construct and operate the prototype reactor. Moreover, not having a strategy for proceeding with Phase 2 could result in the project being on hold indefinitely.

DOE respectfully disagreed with our recommendation that it provide a report to Congress that, among other things, provides initial design parameters or a date for providing them and outlines barriers to proceeding with Phase 2 of the project. DOE stated that such a report was not advisable or useful, or necessary as a means for the Department to comply with the statutory requirements for Phase 1 of the NGNP Project, and further stated that the Department is in compliance with the relevant statutory requirements. As DOE explained, it reported to Congress in 2011 that while it had selected the hydrogen production technology, as required by EPAct 2005, it had not selected the initial design parameters for the project and that based on the recommendations of the Nuclear Energy Advisory Committee, fiscal constraints, competing priorities, projected cost of the prototype, and the inability to reach agreement with industry on cost sharing, it would not proceed with Phase 2 design activities at that time. Instead, it would continue to focus on high-temperature reactor R&D activities and establishment of a public-private partnership, among other things, until conditions warranted a change in direction. DOE did not, however, establish an alternative date for selecting the initial design parameters, as EPAct 2005 required. Rather, it stated that selection of initial design parameters would be made by the public-private partnership once it is formed. Given that almost 3 years have passed since the letter to Congress, we believe that the recommended report is warranted and would serve to inform Congress of the status of the NGNP Project and provide transparency and accountability regarding DOE's intentions for completing Phase 1 and proceeding with Phase 2 of the project. For example, by providing a firm date for selecting the initial design parameters of the NGNP prototype reactor, DOE could be held accountable to meeting that date or could engage in a discussion about whether and why that date should be further extended. Similarly, an updated report to Congress could include a candid description of the ongoing barriers to moving forward, which could spur discussions resulting in legislation or other remedies to mitigate these barriers.

We are sending copies of this report to the Secretary of Energy, the appropriate congressional committees, and other interested parties. In addition, the report is available at no charge on the GAO website at http://www.gao.gov.

If you or your staff members have any questions about this report, please contact Frank Rusco at (202) 512-3841 or ruscof@gao.gov or Dr. Timothy M. Persons at (202) 512-6522 or personst@gao.gov. Contact points for our Offices of Congressional Relations and Public Affairs may be found on the last page of this report. GAO staff who made key contributions to this report are listed in appendix III.

Sincerely yours,

Frank Rusco
Director, Natural Resources and Environment

Timothy M. Persons, Ph.D., Chief Scientist
Director, Center for Science, Technology, and Engineering

Appendix I: Overview of Nuclear Reactor Technologies

Overview of Reactor Operations

Nuclear reactors generate heat by sustaining a fission chain reaction in nuclear fuel. Nuclear fission reactions can occur when a neutron strikes the nucleus of a large atom, causing that nucleus to split, or fission. The result of a fission reaction is typically two fission fragments, or smaller nuclei; 2 or 3 new fast-moving neutrons; and significant heat. In a nuclear reactor, the large atoms used for fission are typically the fissile isotopes uranium-235 or plutonium-239, and the new neutrons produced by a fission reaction are used to initiate new fission reactions, resulting in a sustained fission chain reaction.[1]

This heat generated by this fission reaction is typically used to create steam and drive a steam turbine to generate electricity. Some reactors may also operate at particularly high temperatures and can use the heat to either generate electricity or to supply process heat that can be used for various industrial processes, replacing other heat sources such as natural gas.

Types of Nuclear Reactors

Nuclear reactors typically fall into one of two types based on the neutron spectrum, or neutron energies, at which the fission reactions occur as follows:

- Thermal reactors optimize the fission reaction rate in their fuel. This is done by slowing down, or moderating, the high-energy fast neutrons that are the products of fission reactions. This thermalization of the fast neutrons increases the likelihood that a neutron will initiate a fission reaction. Currently deployed light water reactors, including pressurized water reactors and boiling water reactors, are thermal reactors.
- Fast reactors, by contrast, do not moderate the fission neutrons, leaving them as fast neutrons. A fast neutron has a lower likelihood of initiating a fission event than a slow neutron, so the chain reaction can be more difficult to sustain, but it has the benefit of producing more neutrons when fission does occur. These surplus neutrons, as compared to the number of neutrons produced in thermal reactors, allow fast reactors to be more effective than thermal reactors at

---

[1]Isotopes are varieties of a given chemical element with the same number of protons but different numbers of neutrons. For example, the helium-3 isotope, which is used in research and to detect neutrons in radiation detection equipment, has one less neutron than the helium-4 isotope, which is the helium isotope commonly used in party balloons.

creating, or breeding, new fuel through neutron bombardment of uranium-238 (creating plutonium-239). Fast reactors optimized for fuel production in this manner are called fast breeder reactors and can produce more fuel through breeding than they consume. Fast reactors may also use spent fuel from other nuclear reactors as fuel and thereby reduce long-term fuel disposal needs.

Overview of the Reactor Core

While there are a large number of reactor technologies that can differ significantly, the fission reaction in a reactor occurs in the central region of a reactor called the reactor core. The reactor core typically contains several components as follows:

- **Nuclear fuel.** Nuclear reactors need fissile isotopes, such as uranium-235 and plutonium-239, to sustain chain reactions. Commercial reactors often use uranium ore that has been enriched in the isotope uranium-235 as their fissile fuel; the rest of the fuel consists of the non-fissile uranium-238. However, reactor operation will result in the conversion of some uranium-238 to the fissile isotope plutonium-239, which may then fission and contribute to power generation, and some reactor fuel may start with some of the uranium-235 mixed with plutonium-239 (sometimes referred to as a mixed oxide fuel). Fast reactors can also use spent fuel from other reactors as fuel and can be very effective at converting uranium-238 into plutonium-239. Some reactors can also utilize uranium-233 or thorium-232 as components of their fuel.
- **Moderator.** Thermal reactors use a moderator material to slow down, or thermalize, the fission neutrons in order to sustain the fission reaction. This is needed because neutrons produced by fission reactions are too fast (or energetic) to have a high likelihood of initiating a new fission reaction in fuel. Fast reactors are designed to utilize fast neutrons for the fission reactions and fuel breeding and, as such, do not use a moderator.
- **Coolant.** To remove heat from the core, a coolant—typically water, a gas, or liquid metal—is circulated through the core. The coolant both prevents the core from overheating (which could damage or melt the fuel) and it carries energy, in the form of heat, outside the core for electricity production, typically by generating steam that then drives a steam turbine. In some reactor types, the coolant can also function as the reactor's moderator.
- **Reaction control.** Reactors can use different techniques to maintain the fission chain reaction at appropriate rates. For example, control rods may be inserted into reactor cores to absorb neutrons and slow down (or stop) the chain reaction, or neutron-absorbing materials,

such as boric acid in pressurized water reactors, may be introduced to the coolant system to achieve a similar effect.

Reactor technologies are classified as either thermal or fast reactors (although some technologies are "epithermal" and fall in between the two types) and by the materials used for the moderator or coolant. For example, a pressurized water reactor is a thermal reactor using water as both a coolant and moderator, and a gas-cooled fast reactor is a fast reactor using gas (carbon dioxide or helium) as a coolant.

Table 2 lists and provides information about the reactor types that are either currently operating in the United States or are advanced reactor designs under consideration for development.

Table 2: Characteristics of Commercial Reactor Types, including Those Currently Operating in the United States and Advanced Reactor Designs Under Development

Reactor type (italics indicate current commercial deployment in the United States)	Fuel	Coolant	Moderator	Process heat	Neutron spectrum
Light water reactors • *Pressurized water reactors* • *Boiling water reactors*	Uranium	Water	Water	No	Thermal
Supercritical water cooled reactor	Uranium or mixed oxide	Supercritical water	Supercritical water	Yes	Thermal (may be designed as fast)
High-temperature gas-cooled reactor / very high temperature reactor	Uranium	Helium	Graphite	Yes	Thermal
Liquid-metal-cooled fast reactor • sodium-cooled fast reactor • lead-bismuth cooled fast reactor	Uranium, plutonium, or mixed oxide	Liquid metals (sodium, lead, etc.)	N/A	No	Fast
Gas-cooled fast reactor	Uranium, plutonium, or mixed oxide	Helium or carbon dioxide	N/A	No	Fast
Molten salt reactor or molten salt breeder reactor	Uranium, thorium, or mixed oxide	Molten salts	Graphite (none for breeder)	Yes	Thermal (may be designed as fast)

Sources: GAO analysis of DOE, International Atomic Energy Agency (IAEA), and other documents. | GAO-14-545

Appendix II: Comments from the Department of Energy

Department of Energy
Washington, DC 20585
June 6, 2014

Mr. Frank Rusco
Director, Natural Resources
 and Environment
U.S. Government Accountability Office
441 G Street, NW
Washington, D.C. 20548

Dear Mr. Rusco:

Thank you for providing a draft copy of the Government Accountability Office (GAO) report, "Advanced Reactor Research: DOE Supports Multiple Technologies, but Actions Needed to Ensure a Prototype is Built," (GAO-14-545). We appreciate your thorough review, and we are also pleased that you've acknowledged the Office of Nuclear Energy's critical role in supporting existing light water reactors and a new generation of advanced nuclear reactors.

The draft report is a generally favorable review of NE's approach to advanced reactor R&D and NE's plans and prioritization of its advanced reactor R&D activities. However, the draft report makes two recommendations to better prepare DOE to deploy an advanced reactor through the Next Generation Nuclear Plant (NGNP) project, as established by the Energy Policy Act (EPAct) of 2005. In addition to providing comments on the recommendations in the draft report, we have also provided some clarifying information.

Clarification of Facts

Throughout the document (e.g., pp. 5, 6, 9, 14, 15 and 20) the report uses the term "spent nuclear fuel." For the past decade, DOE has preferred to use the term "used nuclear fuel" to refer to fuel which has been discharged from a light water reactor when it can no longer efficiently produce energy in that type of reactor. At that point, however, approximately 97% of the used fuel's mass still contains fissionable elements which could be reprocessed into new light water reactor fuel or fast reactor fuel.

On page 14, the report discusses the potential economic feasibility of the high temperature gas-cooled reactors (HTGR) and the rationale behind continuing R&D "citing concerns over the reactor's economic viability in relation to the cost of natural gas", the word "current" should be inserted in front of the word "cost" noting that in 2008 natural gas was trading at more than $13 per million BTU compared to today's average of around $4 and that HTGRs are estimated to be competitive against natural gas in the price range of $6 to $8 per million BTU. Given the uncertainty of natural gas prices, the continued long term investment in HTGRs is warranted.

Beginning on page 18, the report contains some mischaracterizations of the Small Modular Licensing Technical Support Program. The first sentence of the second

Printed with soy ink on recycled paper

paragraph should be clarified to indicate that the Department's small modular reactor
programs seek to promote new designs that have advantages over the current fleet of
large light water reactor designs. The sentence that includes, "DOE is supporting first-of-
a-kind engineering development, experiments, and analysis in support of gaining design
certification approval from NRC for the small modular reactors so that construction of a
prototype reactor can begin," should be replaced with, "DOE is supporting design
development, first-of-a-kind engineering, experiments, and analysis in support of gaining
design certification approval from NRC for the small modular reactors so that
commercial deployment of the first SMR can begin."

As currently written, the second paragraph on page 32 indicates that NE decreased its
engagement with the Nuclear Regulatory Commission (NRC), resulting in NRC
reassigning staff from its NGNP work. In fact, the exact opposite has occurred. To date,
NE has maintained an active team which seeks to engage fully with the NRC on NGNP
topics and other advanced reactor licensing issues. However, when NRC received word
that DOE would not proceed to Phase 2 of the NGNP Project, NRC unilaterally chose to
reassign its staff to other projects. Furthermore, the NRC's lack of engagement in this
area has resulted in significant delay in their delivery of several major regulatory
assessment documents which were promised to DOE for delivery in early 2013.

On pages 20 and 22, the report incorrectly states that it is U.S. policy to store used fuel
indefinitely at nuclear power plants. The US has identified its path forward for
addressing used fuel in the 2013 *Strategy for the Management and Disposal of Used Nuclear
Fuel and High-Level Radioactive Waste.* This strategy provides a framework for moving toward
a sustainable program to deploy an integrated system capable of transporting, storing, and
disposing of used nuclear fuel and high-level radioactive waste from civilian nuclear power
generation, defense, national security and other activities. Accordingly, the following sentences
should be revised:

Page 20: Revise the following sentence from:

> *According to NE officials, the development of fast reactors, such as the
> sodium-cooled fast reactor, is likely to play a critical role in managing
> spent nuclear fuel if and when the United States decides to reprocess and
> use its spent nuclear fuel rather than indefinitely store it at reactor sites,
> as is done under current U.S. Policy, or isolate it in a geologic repository
> underground, as has been proposed.*

to:

> *According to NE officials, the development of fast reactors, such as the
> sodium-cooled fast reactor, is likely to play a critical role in managing
> used nuclear fuel if and when the United States decides to reprocess. The
> Administration's current strategy (found here:
> http://energy.gov/downloads/strategy-management-and-disposal-used-*

*nuclear-fuel-and-high-level-radioactive-waste) proposes to move used fuel
from reactor sites to an interim storage facility, for eventual disposal in a
geologic repository underground.*

Page 22: Revise the following sentence from:

*NE officials told us that the current policy of indefinitely storing nuclear
waste in above-ground facilities at nuclear power plants across the
country will eventually be changed, and waste will either be moved to
long-term underground repositories, or reprocessed and burned in fast
nuclear reactors.*

to:

*NE officials told us that the Administration's current strategy (found here:
http://energy.gov/downloads/strategy-management-and-disposal-used-
nuclear-fuel-and-high-level-radioactive-waste) proposes to move used fuel
from reactor sites to an interim storage facility, for eventual disposal in a
geologic repository underground.*

Response to Recommendations:

Recommendation 1: Develop, in consultation with the Nuclear Energy Advisory
Committee and independent nuclear experts, as appropriate, a strategy to proceed with
Phase 2 of the NGNP project, outlining conditions that will warrant a change in program
direction, remaining research and development activities, projected project budget and
schedule, and steps necessary to overcome barriers to successful completion of the
NGNP project.

We agree in principle with the GAO that a strategy to proceed with Phase 2 of the NGNP
project is an important step in the continuation of the NGNP project. The DOE's
responsibilities and authorities include encouraging and conducting research and
development, including demonstration of commercial feasibility and practical
applications of nuclear and other energy sources. Demonstrations can be a useful
element in proving viability of new technologies, but given their high cost, there must be
sufficient government and industry commitment toward deploying commercial
technologies before such demonstrations can be considered. The successful
commercialization of Generation IV reactor technology in the U.S. will require the right
economic and market conditions for manageable financial risk, reduced technical risk,
and establishment of an advanced reactor licensing framework to guide design and
regulatory activities. DOE has performed many analyses of these requirements, and our
current strategy is to continue updating these analyses as needed to reflect changing
market conditions, research and development accomplishments, and the licensing

framework maturity. Any potential future demonstration activities will be evaluated on a
case-by-case basis through budget formulation and the established decision-making
procedures of the Department, including consultation with appropriate advisory bodies
(Nuclear Energy Advisory Committee, National Academies of Science, etc.) and
coordination with the U.S. nuclear industry.

Recommendation 2: Provide a report to Congress complying with the statutory
requirement for Phase 1 of the NGNP project by providing preliminary design parameters
or a date for providing them. The report should also provide an updated status of the
issues DOE identified in its 2011 letter to Congress and outline any additional barriers to
proceeding with Phase 2 of the project, including:

- The status of the establishment of a public-private partnership;
- The project strategy, including conditions that would warrant restarting the
  project; and,
- A legislative proposal, if necessary, to address any barriers to proceeding with the
  project, including the site and cost share requirements.

We respectfully disagree with GAO that such a report to Congress would be advisable or
useful, or that such a report is necessary as a means for the Department to comply with
the statutory requirements for Phase 1 of the NGNP project, as the Department is in
compliance with the relevant statutory requirements.

The Department's October 2011 letter notified Congress that the Department had selected
the hydrogen production technology, as required by EPAct 2005, and acknowledged that
the Department had not selected the initial reactor design parameters for the NGNP. The
letter enclosed the NEAC's report, "Readiness Review of NGNP to Proceed to Phase II of
the Project," submitted in accordance with EPAct 2005, which concluded the Project was
not ready for a decision to proceed to the complete set of Phase 2 activities. Based on the
NEAC recommendations in accordance with EPAct 2005, fiscal constraints, competing
priorities, projected cost of the prototype, and inability to reach agreement with industry
on cost sharing, DOE reported to Congress in 2011 that the Department would not
proceed with the Phase 2 design activities at that time, but would continue to focus on
high temperature reactor research and development activities, interactions with the
Nuclear Regulatory Commission to develop a licensing framework, and establishment of
a public-private partnership until conditions warranted a change in direction. DOE also
set up a process to select the initial reactor design parameters, stating that selection of
initial design parameters would be made by the public-private partnership once it is
formed. The information provided to Congress in the October 2011 letter is fully
compliant with the EPAct requirements in section 645 for Phase 1 of the NGNP project.
The Department will continue to provide information to, and work with Congress,
industry and other interested stakeholders with respect to its activities in the area of high
temperature reactor research and development.

If you have any questions, please contact me or Mr. Thomas J. O'Connor, Director for
the Office of Advanced Reactor Technologies Program Manager, at 301-903-6781.

Sincerely,

Peter B. Lyons,
Assistant Secretary,
 for Nuclear Energy

Appendix III: GAO Contacts and Staff Acknowledgments

GAO Contacts	Frank Rusco, (202) 512-3841 or ruscof@gao.gov Timothy M. Persons, (202) 512-6522 or personst@gao.gov
Staff Acknowledgments	In addition to the contacts named above, Ned Woodward (Assistant Director), John Barrett, Elizabeth Beardsley, John Delicath, R. Scott Fletcher, Cindy Gilbert, Michael Krafve, Tom Lombardi, Mehrzad Nadji, and Kiki Theodoropoulos made key contributions to this report.